I0063056

Banner Ads

B. Vincent

Published by RWG Publishing, 2021.

While every precaution has been taken in the preparation of this book, the publisher assumes no responsibility for errors or omissions, or for damages resulting from the use of the information contained herein.

BANNER ADS

First edition. June 16, 2021.

Copyright © 2021 B. Vincent.

Written by B. Vincent.

Also by B. Vincent

Table of Contents

Banner Ads

Hello, and welcome to this course on Banner Advertising. In this course we're going to cover how to drive traffic with banner advertising. This course is divided into three modules:

1. Module one covers creating banner ads;
2. Module two covers ad campaign goals; and
3. Module three cover setting up and running the campaign.

By the time this course is over you'll know how to effectively create and run banner ad campaigns for your business. So without further ado, let's dive into the first module.

Module One

Okay, guys, welcome to Module One. In this module, our expert will be teaching you about designing the actual banner ads. So get ready to take some notes and let's jump right in.

Alright guys. So we are inside of Bannersnack and this is what we're going to create our ad words, banner ad. Now there's two options here. Single banner and banner set. Banner set is an incredibly useful tool that you need to be aware of. It can really decrease the amount of time that you spend trying to customize all the different dimensions and sizes of banners. You just grabbed your main elements. So your main image and your headline, and maybe a little bit more text, and then you create one ad and then it automatically creates all the rest of those ads and all the different dimensions. The sidebar dimension, the header dimension, the perfect square dimension, the smaller perfect square dimension. You understand what I'm saying? And all you do is you go through after its auto generated those and you'd click and drag things around a little bit. It's an incredibly useful tool.

Now, to keep things simple for the purpose of this lesson, we're just going to make a single banner ad to use inside of the Google Display Network Ads Platform. So let's go with a standard large rectangle. Now, there's a ton of great templates to work with and to start with, we're going to skip these. And of course there's some seasonal ones here taking up most of the queue. We're going to go ahead and create our own. So I'm going to come over here to add image. I'm going to grab this image of a gal over here put it right there. We're going to scale her a little bit. So she takes up a little bit less space.

There we go. Almost perfect. Okay. And that gives us a little bit of room for a headline above her. Let's add some text. Because of the size of the ad, we'll just use the sub-headline size. And we're going to say just for grins, that we're selling some type of a tooth whitening kit. Okay. So let's actually put the word overnight there. We'll grab a larger headline text. We'll put whiter teeth overnight and let's give it a little bit of color blue and some red. Whiter teeth overnight, pretty straightforward standard toothpaste ad. These have not changed very much in the last 200 years or so I don't think. let's see. So everything jives here. Okay. This is a good square banner ad. We've got a smiling woman with white teeth. We've got the headline whiter teeth overnight. And we would presumably be sending someone when they click on this to a landing page for a free trial kit or something like that. If we were doing a loss-leader thing or we could send them directly to a sales page or an e-commerce store or something along those lines so that we can get them into our funnel and offer them our solution.

So I'm going to go ahead and hit save, and we'll call this teeth zero one and let's see, let's save again. And this time, what we'll do is we'll download the PNG. So now we'll come over here to Google Ad Words, and we're going to click on, let's go to campaigns, new campaign, and now we need to pick a goal for this campaign, which is what we'll do in the next lesson.

Module Two

Hey folks, welcome to Module Two. In this module, our expert will be covering Ad Campaign Goals. So get ready to take some notes and let's jump right in.

Alright. So we're here where we left off in the last lesson at the campaign page. Basically what Google ads has done and most of the major ad platforms have done this as well is they want to take users and have them choose an overarching overall campaign goal before they start creating their ad. And then throughout the process, based on the goal that they choose, they're going to get little hints and little taylorism to sort of help them accomplish what they're trying to. It's a pretty smart move, and it makes it much more accessible to your average Joe, who would sometimes just play with these different ad platforms and not have any success and then give up. So this is definitely a move in the right direction. Let's go through each of these goals and see which ones are relevant to us since we're running a display ad campaign.

So first off sales drive. Sales online and app by phone or in store, that's pretty straightforward, right? You're either going to be sending somebody to a sales page or to an e-commerce store, and you can also do it via app and phone with the phone numbers inside of the ads, which is kind of cool. And it looks like campaign types, search display, and shopping are associated with this. So this could be an option for us.

Next one leads. Get leads and other conversions by encouraging customers to take an action, pretty straightforward, sending people to landing pages, right? Campaign types, search display, shop, video, website traffic. Get people to visit your website the most basic, you know straightforward one out there. A little bit overused, I would say generally speaking you should be choosing one of these two, if you're just moving website traffic, but if you're just doing content marketing or something like that, this could be a good option. Search display, shopping video, once again are the associated campaign types that you can choose from if you choose this as your goal.

Product and brand consideration. Now, this is an interesting one. This is where you can actually get some complex ads that allow users to sort of explore the different features of products or services and allows them to sort of compare yours to other offerings out there. It does work with display and with video.

Brand awareness and reach. This is less about people clicking and actually taking an action and more about just getting your brand identity, your visual brand identity and name out there in front of as many eyeballs as possible. So it's mostly focused on impressions, not clicks, not conversions, but impressions. Okay. So that subconsciously people start becoming more aware of your brand because they're seeing it everywhere, whether or not they're actually, you know, typing into a form or buying your stuff at that moment. So campaign types for this, as you can imagine, display is in fact, one of them and video is the other.

App promotion. That's exactly, it sounds like, and you're trying to get installs interactions for your mobile app and creates a campaign without a goals, guidance. You should really stay away from this one, unless you're kind of an ads guru and you know everything about this, you know, the bidding, you know, the auction concept, you know conversions, you know, all the different algorithms and variables and elements involved, and you understand how it works. And you want to just sort of go in there and do everything on your own. This is the option for you, but it's not a particularly smart one if you're not an absolute AdWords guru. So it's better to pick one of these. And I think for us, we're just going to send people straight to a sales page for our teeth whitening solution.

Let's click on this. We're going to choose display. We could choose shopping if we're sending them to an e-commerce store or something like that. That's definitely an option. We'll just do a standard display ad this time though. And standard display ad campaign, Gmail campaign. That's a pretty cool concept as well, sending people or showing people ads within their free Gmail accounts we'll stick with standard display campaigns. So we can you know, show up and pop up on websites all over the web while people are browsing. We'll go to what we will say whiteteeth.com, which I don't even know if that is a website am just typing it in (inaudible 08:47) continue. And this brings us into the actual process of setting up the campaign, which is what we'll start getting into more in the next lesson.

Module Three

*A*lright, welcome to module three. In this module, our expert will be covering, setting up and running the campaign. So get ready to take some notes and let's jump right in.

Alright. So here we are on the actual campaign settings page. We're going to go through the process of setting up and running and launching our campaign here. Now, the first thing you might notice is this number right here, our targeting reach as far as impressions is 10 billion plus. Why? Because we haven't set any categories to narrow down our audience yet. So right here in location, language and down here in the audience section, we'll start narrowing that number down. Maybe, maybe not as much as you think though, because it's teeth whitening. It's not really super specific to any demographic. It's not really super specific to any niche or any hobby or any area of interest. Everybody for the most part has teeth. So we might end up leaving this pretty broad. Now, let's say we're going to operate inside the United States only so we won't mess with the location at all. Although if you really wanted to, you could add cities, zip codes, states in here, you could even go to advanced search and you could narrow in on one little neighborhood.

Let's say you were a door to door teeth whitening kit salesman, and you want to you know, do some local area stuff, generate leads in the local area. You could drop a pin right there inside of Lexington, you know, and or let's say, you know, this whole area here and adjust the radius a little bit and target anybody within 10 nautical miles of let's say Shelbyville and Waddy in Kentucky there. So you can get pretty advanced with the locations. We're not going to do that though. Okay. It's teeth whitening kits. We're mailing them out to people. Okay. In our little pretend scenario and we'll just leave it to the United States at large.

Let's come down here, languages. We'll just stick with English because the ad is written in English. And language doesn't really have any more of an impact on our product or our ad. We want to focus on high quality traffic right here, or we could focus on clicks and impressions. Now, honestly, if we're selling things and we're not really selling anything super expensive traffic quality doesn't really matter too much for something as basic as what we're doing. We're selling a normal priced teeth whitening kit. Okay. Now, if we were sort of trying to qualify leads, you know, and then sending them into an appointment settings apparatus or something like that, that would be more inclined to focus on high quality traffic. But I think everybody wants white teeth. And so we're going to focus on clicks in our case. Okay. There's a bunch of other things you can choose here by the way.

Sometimes depending on what type of ad you selected you'll see conversion of value, or just plain conversions here. In this case, it's grayed out because we haven't set up conversion tracking as another feature within our AdWords account. But if you were to do that, you would be able to optimize here for conversions, which used to be the language, which by the way. If you're wondering where that went, it's no longer, what do you want to optimize for it's what do you want to focus on. Which I think was just a marketing decision made at AdWords. If you wanted to, you could manually set bids, I'm going to set it to automatically maximum clicks so that we're allowing Google and its algorithms to do all the work. And we're going to just see after running that for a while, if we're happy with the results that we get, if we're not, we can always change it to manual, but let's trust Google, the almighty Google, and their algorithms for awhile.

And we're not going to set a CPC bid limit because this is our first campaign for this product. Again, make believe here. And we just want to see what happens first, and then we'll adjust bid limits or manual bidding later on if we want to. But if you, if you wanted to, you could set this at $1 and as you can see here, it won't go beyond that bidding per click. And when we talk about bidding, we're utilizing the old standard auction strategy, which is very you know, complex concept, it's difficult to understand, but you're basically letting the algorithm take over and you're letting the algorithm know, Hey, this is what I'm willing to bid. Okay. We're paying for clicks every time somebody clicks, we're paying for a click to our to our sales page.

And let's see here budget. Now, this is important. Okay. Budget does not mean a cap on what you will spend each day. Okay. It does not mean a cap. What it does is it takes the average, it says, enter the average you want to spend each day. So whatever number you put here, it'll take that number. And it'll basically average it out over the course of 30 days. So that's you will not have spent more than that number of times about 30. Does that kind of make sense? So if you put 10 in here, you can expect about $300 to have been spent by the end of the month. Okay. And on Monday you might've only spent $5 on Tuesday you might spend 20. Okay. It's important to understand that this could be double every day you could spend double what you actually put in this line here. Okay. But the average over time, after 30 days will end up being this number times 30. Okay.

So it's kind of complicated. It's a little bit confusing and misleading, but just understand that's what you're doing. So basically come up with a monthly budget, divide it by 30 and put it right here. Okay. I don't even know why they, why they choose to structure it this way. It's a little bit confusing, but that's what you're doing. A monthly budget divided by 30. And that's approximately what you're going to put right here. So let's go ahead and say that we're willing to spend, oh, I don't know, $100 up to a $100 per day, or you know, roughly $3,000 per month.

Delivery method. If you want it to - if you were on a tight timeline you could set accelerated and it'll spend your money faster and get your ads in front of more people and get more clicks in a shorter period of time. In our case, we don't have, you know, really a tight timeline. You know, we don't have a sales quota to meet by the end of the month. We don't have a specific product launch that ends on a given day. We don't have a live event or anything. We're not bound by the calendar and people's teeth are not going anywhere. So we can just stick to the standard method here, add group name, auto-generate add group one, we'll stick with that.

And then here, we've got audiences. Now, audiences, if you have a very specific type of product in a certain niche, you'd be doing a lot of poking around in here. In our case again it's a teeth whitening solution. So it's our best interests to keep this relatively broad, but just for grins so you can see what could be researched in here.

Let's poke around a little bit and let's theorize that maybe people interested in beauty and wellness would be more likely to click on this ad. And we could always do another campaign later or just choose one ad group within this campaign that focuses on that target and see if in fact we do get better results that way, but we could do this. Okay. And that would basically you know, narrow down the audience a little bit from super broad to less broad. For our purposes, we'll go ahead and keep it. We'll go ahead and keep it as it is without any specific audience restrictions.

Demographics. Honestly, we could sit here, do some research and maybe find out that females are more likely to buy this, which sounds right, when I say it that sounds like something that your average person would think. We don't know that. And oftentimes when you actually do your market research, you'll find out that the reality is different from conventional wisdom. But yeah, we could do research that gives us actual demographic results. In fact, any time you run an ad campaign, you should have sat down and done some market research and figured out what's called an Ideal Customer Avatar, okay. Where you're actually saying, Hey, our ideal customer, the most likely one to purchase is between 35 and 54, you know, and they're female, right. And their parents and their household income, you know, is in the top 30% or higher. Okay. Now, that's that I think really applies to us too much for this example. Number one, because we're pretending to be a teeth whitening company. So we don't actually have the audience data more importantly though, again, everybody's got teeth. So I think for our first ad ever in the history of our teeth whitening company, we'll leave it pretty broad and then analyze the results afterwards. Okay.

It's time to create the ad. Let's click down here and we'll click on upload display ads. And final URL for that is whiteteeth.com. Like we chose earlier, I'll click choose files to upload, go ahead and grab our neat little white teeth overnight ad and click add to ad group. And there we go. We've got our and campaign ready to be started. Create campaign, click it twice there. And this is a quick summary of all the details of our campaign. Okay. So we can review all the choices that we made. Again, we left it pretty broad. So there's nothing super interesting here, except for a reminder of course, the daily budget. Click continue and there we are now, here's what you want to pay attention to when you're monitoring your campaign after it's launched clicks, impressions, click through rate and average cost per click. So clicks, obviously somebody clicking impression means all the people who saw it loaded on their browser at one point, whether they noticed it or not, that's why it's called, you know impressions instead of sightings. A lot of people don't even know this ads, right? They have banner blindness, but it was loaded. There's an instance of it being loaded in someone's browser that equals one impression. Okay.

So clicks, impressions, click through rate would be what percentage of the impressions of people who technically, you know, quote unquote saw it ended up clicking. Okay. And that's your click through rate.

And then average cost per click is basically the total cost that you've spent to get that number of clicks that equals your average cost per click. Okay. So that's what you want to monitor. We don't really have much to compare it to right now. And of course at the moment, we don't have any data whatsoever to look at, but you would want to monitor those, compare them to past campaigns, if you do have past campaigns. And also obviously the big thing to compare it to here is when you send someone into your funnel, your teeth whitening kit funnel, how much money are you making? What's the average customer value, the lifetime customer value, as well as the initial order value. And if those numbers don't jive, meaning if the expense per click outweighs the average amount that you make from bringing on a customer, obviously you need to get back into that campaign settings page and start tweaking things a little bit and try to get that number down as much as possible.

But that's it guys we've gone through the whole process of creating a visual nice display ad setting it up with all the various parameters and finally launching it.

Don't miss out!

Visit the website below and you can sign up to receive emails whenever B. Vincent publishes a new book. There's no charge and no obligation.

https://books2read.com/r/B-A-QWUO-OFPPB

BOOKS 2 READ

Connecting independent readers to independent writers.

Also by B. Vincent

About the Publisher

Accepting manuscripts in the most categories. We love to help people get their words available to the world.

Revival Waves of Glory focus is to provide more options to be published. We do traditional paperbacks, hardcovers, audio books and ebooks all over the world. A traditional royalty-based publisher that offers self-publishing options, Revival Waves provides a very author friendly and transparent publishing process, with President Bill Vincent involved in the full process of your book. Send us your manuscript and we will contact you as soon as possible.

Contact: Bill Vincent at rwgpublishing@yahoo.com www.rwgpublishing.com

www.ingramcontent.com/pod-product-compliance
Lightning Source LLC
Chambersburg PA
CBHW030537210326
41597CB00014B/1184